THE HERO IN YOU

120+ POWER TIPS FOR WRITERS

Manna Ko

*International Speaker and Author of
Made For More™*

© 2018 Manna Ko

Made For More™, Manna For Life® are unregistered and registered trademarks of The Manna Ko Group Inc. in the United States and/or other countries. All other trademarks cited herein are the property of their respective owners.

No part of this publication may be reproduced, distributed, or transmitted in any form or by any means, including photocopying, recording, or other electronic or mechanical methods, without the prior written permission of the publisher, except in the case of brief quotations embodied in critical reviews and certain other noncommercial uses permitted by copyright law.

For permission requests, write to Covenant and Gate, 2683 Via De La Valle, Suite G523, Del Mar, California, USA. 92014

PRINT ISBN-13: 978-1-943060-12-2 (ISBN-10: 1-943060-12-6)
EBOOK ISBN-13: 978-1-943060-13-9 (ISBN-10: 1-943060-13-4)

All scripture quotations, unless otherwise indicated, are taken from the Holy Bible, New International Version®, NIV®. Copyright ©1973, 1978, 1984, 2011 by Biblica, Inc.™ Used by permission of Zondervan. All rights reserved worldwide. www.zondervan.com The "NIV" and "New International Version" are trademarks registered in the United States Patent and Trademark Office by Biblica, Inc.™ NKJV Scripture taken from the New King James Version®. Copyright © 1982 by Thomas Nelson. Used by permission. All rights reserved. Scripture quotations marked (NLT) are taken from the Holy Bible, New Living Translation, copyright ©1996, 2004, 2007, 2013 by Tyndale House Foundation. Used by permission of Tyndale House Publishers, Inc., Carol Stream, Illinois 60188. All rights reserved. Scripture quotations from THE MESSAGE. Copyright © by Eugene H. Peterson 1993, 1994, 1995, 1996, 2000, 2001, 2002. Used by permission of Tyndale House Publishers, Inc.

All rights reserved.

ALSO BY MANNA KO

Books

Made For More™
Know Your More. Own Your More. Live Your More.™
Know Your More. Own Your More. Live Your More.™ Journal
I Am Made For More™
Your Made For More Journey™
My Spiritual First Aid Kit for Women
My Spiritual First Aid Kit for Men
Chopsticks and Chocolate Chips
Feeding Families and Friends
Feeding Our 4-Legged Families and Friends

Courses

You're Made For More™
Know Your More. Own Your More. Live Your More.™
MORE Than Words
The Hero In You
Redeem The Dream

CONTENTS

	Acknowledgment	i
	Dedication	ii
	Introduction	iii
1	Find Your Purpose	Page 1
2	Focused And Motivated	Page 8
3	Power Up	Page 12
4	Honesty And Grace	Page 20
5	Look After Yourself!	Page 36
6	Look After Your Technology.	Page 40
7	Now What?	Page 42
8	Keep Going	Page 45

ACKNOWLEDGMENTS

Thank you, IGBE.

DEDICATION

To Miss Marsh, Mrs. Glazier, and Mr. Morris.

I will never be able to thank you enough for believing in me and stopping at nothing to teach me well.

INTRODUCTION

Your gifts will find you.
Yes, your gifts will find you.

Regardless of how far I fell (or ran) astray from my calling, somehow my gifts always found me.

When I was a little girl, I didn't know how to dream. I didn't know how to think about my future because I saw none.

As a child I heard, "You're stupid, ugly, and good for nothing," multiple times per day, every day. It was one of the many negative mantras from my mother and stepfather. As a result, I started to believe it was true.

It wasn't until the age of 14, when the courts said my brother and I could move in with my father, that I actually started to believe something different.

I dared to believe for *more*.

By this time, my friends were starting to plan for university, and enrolling in courses they knew would prepare them for their future. They knew their giftings and talents, and they were engaged in developing them.

Sadly, I knew none of that. I had no idea what I wanted for my future because I had lived so long not knowing if I would have one.

"But God…"

God directed my steps, somehow. I found myself not only enrolled for the mandatory English classes, I also signed up for all the elective English courses as well. I didn't have a plan. I was just following unseen orders that carried me from one class to the next.

At first, my writing was mediocre, but because I had some amazing teachers who encouraged me and believed in me, I started to excel in my classes.

Miss. Marsh, Mrs. Glazier, and Mr. Morris (my favorite and the best teacher I've ever had), instructed me as if I was their chosen apprentice. They were warm, patient, and firm. They didn't care about my awkwardness or the color of my skin, no matter how difficult racism was in those days.

They saw "me," and called out the best in me.

I learned to write with those great mentors and before I knew it, I was enrolled in university, majoring in English and Psychology, and you guessed it—writing a lot!

Still not fully knowing how to dream, I was at least open to it at that point and set my sights on pre-Law. Unfortunately, I never did end up pursuing Law as a career, but I did achieve my Master's Degree in Psychology and my PhD in philosophy.

Yes, more writing!

I share this with you because I want you to know, even if you don't think you have gifts, were told you had none, or were too afraid to dream, God has something bigger in store.

You were *MADE FOR MORE™!*

He has great and mighty plans for you! "No eye has seen, no ear has heard, and no mind has imagined what God has prepared for those who love him."[i]

So now you understand.

Your gifts will find you.

Now, many years later, I have written hundreds of curricula, articles, business manuals, over a dozen books, and in the Fall of 2018, I will be releasing a children's book series.

Never doubt that God has great and mighty plans for you, my friend! No matter what you've been through (or are going through), *your gifts will find you.*

And this is exactly where this book comes in.

My intention was not to write a comprehensive "how to write" book. There are plenty of great books like these out there.

My assignment in writing this book is simple; to provide you with a fun resource of speedy reminders to encourage you to stay the course.

The items I share below are some of the effective strategies I used to publish my books, and I am confident they will help you publish yours, too.

I've shared these *POWER* tips with every writer's group I speak at because they are proven, and I want to share these same tips with you now.

Many of the ideas will seem so basic, you may find yourself saying something like "duh!" But I can't tell you how often (when I give these tips) people say, "Oh, I get it!" And, inevitably, they finish their writing projects.

Paraphrasing Einstein, genius is making the complex simple - and that is what I've tried to do here. Keep things simple (yet still effective) to encourage you.

Some of the tips I'll also be sharing are amazing quotes that I wouldn't presume to add commentary to. Their brilliance and impact stand on their own. Let them "do their thing" to inspire you.

Lastly, since this is not your typical book, you may want to read it like a resources book – going to sections that will be most helpful to you as you are writing. That said, you may also want to enjoy it over to cover. Lots of people have written to say they have.

I pray these tips will bless you and encourage you.

Congratulations on your writer's journey!

Your gifts have found you.

Blessings,
Manna
June 2018
San Diego, CA

THE HERO IN YOU

120+ Power Tips for Writers

1

FIND YOUR PURPOSE

"Memories are the key not to the past, but to the future."
Corrie Ten Boom

1. How will you know for certain that you're supposed to write? And/or how do you know you're supposed to tell your story?

- The answer should be something like, "You feel as though a part of you would die if you didn't write - if you didn't tell your story."

2. Pray.

- When you lift anything up in prayer, both you and your writing rise to a higher perspective. Why? Because you're seeing things from a higher level. Not only can you write with more clarity and wisdom, you're able to write with more efficiency and effectiveness.

- Revisit your purpose often. It will be both your rudder and your compass.

3. Check your heart.

- What is your intention in writing your story or project?
    - If you write to encourage, inspire, and to liberate others, then that's awesome.
    - If you're writing to retaliate for a wounded past, then go back to tip 2 before proceeding.

4.   Do everything with love.

5.   Be gentle with others, and yourself.

- Memories will stir other memories. Breathe.
- Forgive those who didn't know better, including yourself. Breathe.

6.   Write with the heart of the reader in mind.

- What you may be sharing could be difficult to read. Always keep this in mind. You hold your readers' hearts in your hand, so you must write your story in a way that you will bring them into heartbreak, through it, and out into the sunshine afterward.

- In a word, each story you tell must be *redemptive.* There must be a bigger picture and a bigger story; a story greater than your situation. What did you learn? How does what

you write help others learn? Overcome? Grow? Have hope? Transform?
- Your reader must be able to feel your pain but not be traumatized by it.

7. Write when you aren't distracted by other priorities.

- Always work on your life priorities first – family, work projects, etc.
- Honor your agreements with others. Then, when you are in your writing zone, you'll write with a clean heart and a free mind, knowing you did what you said you were going to do.

8. When you start writing, don't let emails, calls, anything, or anyone distract you.

- Write with your email notifications off and your phone silent (or in another room).

9. Keep a notepad and a pen with you throughout the day.

- Jot down every random idea and memory that comes to mind.
- Make notes as often as necessary. Return to them when you have time.

- If you're driving and an idea comes to mind, DO NOT WRITE in your notepad! When you stop at your destination, then write your idea down, or record it on your phone.

10. Tell stories only you can tell.

- Yes, there will always be stronger, smarter, wittier, funnier, more poetic, and overall better writers than you…but only YOU can be YOU. And only YOU can tell the stories that YOU know.
- Write what you know. Write "you!"
- This kind of writing is much more credible, relational, trust-building, community-driven and life-changing anyway.

11. Write from a thankful place in your heart.

- This will radically change your perspective, attitude, creativity, and IMPACT!

12. Write from your place of insight—let it be an "offering."

- With practice, you can even do this in non-fiction and "how-to" books.

"Writing is not an event; it's who you are. Your books may be events, but writing is a way of life."
							Manna Ko

13. Commit to your writing and take it seriously.

- You won't hear your mother or father telling you to practice your writing in the same way they would about practicing the piano, violin, or your swing at golf. Nor will they take you to the computer to improve your craft like they would take you to tennis lessons to master your serve, or basketball courts to master your free throws. This is your "thing." Own it. Master it.

14. Be generous with your writing.

- Leave it all on the table. Give it your absolute best on the first draft *and* on the 12th rewrite. You have one chance to make a great impression, so be generous in your writing beforehand.
- Be daring, courageous and bold.
- This isn't about perfection, this is all (*and only*) about the heart.

"Technique and style may carry you from page to page, but courageous content will carry you to the reader's heart."
Manna Ko

15. Believe in yourself when no one else does.

16. The words don't always flow, but they will. Be patient. Keep writing.

17. You won't always be confident, or enjoy writing.

- Be patient.
- Keep writing.
- You will be so thankful you pushed on.
- If in doubt, review these points again.

Some encouraging words from Maya Angelou:

"There is no greater agony than bearing an untold story inside you."

"The idea is to write it so that people hear it and it slides through the brain and goes straight to the heart."

"The more you know of your history, the more liberated you are."

"Hold those things that tell your history and protect them. During slavery, who was able to read or write or keep anything? The ability to have somebody to tell your story to is so important. It says: 'I was here. I may be sold tomorrow, but you know I was here.'"

"I promised myself that I would write as well as I can, tell the truth, not to tell everything I know, but to make

sure that everything I tell is true, as I understand it. And to use the eloquence which my language affords me."

2

FOCUSED AND MOTIVATED

"Writing is a solitary occupation. Family, friends, and society are the natural enemies of the writer. He must be alone, uninterrupted, and slightly savage if he is to sustain and complete and undertaking."

Jessamyn West

18. Have a very strong heart for your project.

- If you are called to tell your story, be committed and unwavering.
- Finish well. Finish strong.

19. Know your vision.

- Own it. And work it. Your vision to write a book will be hard work, but it will be worth it.

20. Know your strengths.

- Work and use them well.
- Know your weaknesses. Get support.
- Join forces with a writing coach or a mentor.

- Do your research.
- Hire a great editor (will explain more later).

21. Make an agreement with loved ones that when you're writing, you're focused and not to be interrupted.

- You're not being anti-social or rude, you're simply moving a mountain and you need to concentrate.

22. Plan family times or date nights with your loved ones.

- They deserve something nice since they're patiently "tolerating" you during this process.

23. Designate a "creativity cave" or "scribe's sanctuary".

- This is your own private space where you'll be doing your writing. As soon as you enter this area, you'll know you are in the "writing zone".

24. Protect your time and space when you write, no matter where it is.

- Writing means you're going to create. If you don't like doing this work from home, then arrange a time to create in a public space (coffee shop, restaurant, park, etc.). Just remember, you're not there to socialize. You're there to write.

25. Have a great support team beside you; loved ones you can talk to (spouse, friends, mentor, counselor, pastor, etc.).

26. Everyone wants to glamorize and romanticize writing—don't do it.

- Writing can be hard work at times. Sometimes it'll flow like a fire hose. Other times, you'll feel like you're in a writing draught. Press on.
- Writing takes commitment, sacrifice, a strong heart and tough skin.
- Writing is like breathing. You have to breathe. You have to write.

27. Be willing to be responsible and accountable for your writing and yourSELF.

- Start by being aware, conscious and yes, even mature.
- The more you take your writing seriously, the more fun you'll have with it.

"For who will testify, who will accurately describe our lives if

we do not do it ourselves?"

Faye Moskowitz

3

POWER UP

28. Get a 12-month calendar (preferably one of the laminated ones) and put it on a wall that you can see every day.

- Set a finish date for your project and write it on your calendar.
- Work backward to schedule your writing goals.
- Your work may not take 12 months, or it could take longer, depending on the scope of your project. Either way, note it on your wall calendar so you can start managing your goals and time commitments well.

29. Keep a 90-day planner for your bigger goals.

- For example:
    - Finish 3 chapters by May 1st
    - Consolidate and confirm your references

30. Keep a 30-day planner for your smaller goals.

- For example:
    - Finish writing sections in Chapter 1
    - Develop a particular character

31. Have at least 3-5 priorities in your planner going all the time. It's a great way to stay focused and on task.

32. Keep a weekly and a daily planner.

- This is for prioritizing other important daily life routines and goals so you know how to prioritize time to go into your writing zone.

33. Keep a journal/computer doc that no one reads but you.

- Write down everything you think about life, yourself, situations, the people around you, work, dreams, frustrations, things you don't understand, fears, worries, imaginations, venting…
- Don't edit it or censor it. Just write your thoughts down, especially if you're going through a tough season.

- You'll want to do this because it's important to get out anything that distracts you from your task at hand - writing.

34. Have a separate document open called "Extra Writings."

- This is separate from #33 (your journal where you write your feelings, etc.). In this document, you'll write different scenes or ideas when they suddenly pop up. And *trust me* – they will pop up. You'll be working fine, and then suddenly, you'll want to write about something else. It may be relevant to your work, but not necessarily a part of that particular section. Just write it all down in "Extra Writings". You can add headers to each "random" paragraph or excerpt so you can find it later, but this writing space is definitely something you're going to want to have available to you.

- When I'm writing, I may have eight or more documents opened at one time. I'm not saying this is the best way to do it, but I am saying "I understand" when things come up. Sometimes, your mind is in a groove and when there's flow, you will want a place to record your overflowing genius safely.

35. Use Microsoft® Word for now.

- Unless you are a professional writer/author, I would highly recommend you save money (and the effort you'll spend on the learning curves), and just use MS WORD for now. When you finish your manuscript, and are on to your next project, then you can consider other writing platforms.

- I'm not an affiliate for them.
- If you are already having success with another platform, then stick with it.

36. Use emotions to write.

- The only way a reader is going to fall in love with your writing is if they can "get you" – that is, if you make your characters and your scenes, "real." To do that, you're going to need to write vulnerably, raw, and sometimes, even feel naked. That's good. Very good. Don't settle for less.

37. Keep all your journal writings.

- You'll be amazed at how far you've come when you review your work one day.

38. Write something every day.

- Write, even if it's in your journal/word doc, and even if it's only for 30 minutes. Write.
- You can't be a good writer if you don't keep practicing your craft.

39. Join a writing group and/or critique group.

- You can get help from your writing peers. They will give you great feedback, ideas, resources and practice. Don't be afraid to share your work and ask for help in this group.
- Some writing groups will give you great tools, exercises and have guest speakers who you can also learn a lot from.
- Some writing groups are online, so look around to find the best one for you.

40. Attend writing workshops and retreats.

41. Read great books about writing techniques.

42. Keep things simple.

- Especially with vocabulary, unless it is in line with one of your characters etc.
- As a general rule, don't force yourself to use "big" vocabulary words. People can tell when you're being inauthentic and puffing. Remember, people want "real."

- There is a fine line between stretching yourself and puffery. The former will develop with your maturity as a writer. The latter will demonstrate arrogance and haughtiness. I've stopped reading books when I saw the author puffing up.
- Plots can be complex but they don't have to be complicated.
- Keep things simple.

43. Go to places that inspire you.

- Your writing environment is very important. Protect this place as your writing sanctuary. See Chapter 2.
- For practice and to warm up, write about what you see there; a pebble, a bench, people chatting at the coffee table, the teacup, anything.
- Have a writing session in your journal or word document.
- Then, work on your book.

44. Don't call yourself a writer. Call yourself an author.

- The latter will do 2 things:
  1) Remind you of your calling

2) If you aren't published yet, the dissonance of calling yourself "an author" will stir the juices inside you so that you get to business.

45. Don't be afraid of making mistakes.

- It's part of learning.
- It happens to everyone in every field, even the masters.
- You're not supposed to be perfect.
- Make the mistakes, and learn from them.
- Every line you write is practice for the next line.
- Instead of using the word "mistake," use the word, "practice," instead.

46. If your work doesn't seem to fit into stereotypical genres, make up your own.

- Don't worry. The same thing happened to me.
- I was turned down by several publishers because they didn't know what category/genre to put my work. So, I created my own.
- I created the Autobiographical Novel genre.
- Someone else created Speculative Memoir.
- If your work is different than a typical genre, don't worry. Keep writing. Either one will fit perfectly for you by the time you're finished, or you can be a pioneer and create your own.

Inspiring quotes to encourage you:

"Definition of failure: having a dream and letting fear steal it." Manna Ko

"Be unkind to your characters when you are exploring who they are. Challenge them, put them in difficult situations and see how they respond, present them with strong choices and show us their development. Interrogate them. Do they have any transgressions? Once you see the world from your characters' point of view, their emotional logic will be authentic."

Jenny Downham

4

HONESTY AND GRACE

"A memoir isn't the summary of a life; it's a window into a life, very much like a photograph in its selective composition. It may look like a casual and even random calling up of bygone events. It's not; it's a deliberate construction."
William Zinsser

47. Dig deep.

- Don't worry about editing or censoring your work when you start. Do your best, and just keep writing.

48. Tell the truth.

- Be honest but not cruel, especially in an autobiography. There are ways to tell harsh and painful experiences without being cruel. See Chapter 1.

- It's challenging but it can be done.

49. Write from your perspective but give the reader insight into what could have

been going on in the backstory of others around you.

- It shows you were courageous enough to have done the personal work necessary for writing these difficult experiences responsibly. It shows you have maturity, and it shows you are wise enough to extend compassion to you – and to others.

50. Show *and* tell.

- Strong writers show the reader what's going on little by little. Don't just tell them. Let them visualize each scene and trust your reader to "get it".

- There will be times you have to "tell it as it is," and that's fine. Just notice which is most suitable and when it's most applicable. Write accordingly.

51. Take your reader on a journey and let the story unfold.

- Meander, then go around a corner, then throw in a surprise before traveling onto another path. Take your reader on a journey so each mile marker engages them so much, they are compelled to finish the book

52. Love your reader.

- Your reader isn't just some random person you want to just drag into your fight with "life." Think of them as your "friends."
- When you write, write as though you love your reader. They deserve your attention, your respect, and your best.
- Ask yourself: If you were a reader, how would you feel reading what you wrote?

53. Start with an outline.

- Take your time with this.
- You may revise it a few times before you actually get writing.
- Sometimes you revise your outline as you write because a better path is revealed to you.
- Review your outline often.
- Remember, you may feel inspired to write different parts of your book at different times. If you have an outline, you'll know where to place/categorize the work you just finished in the right place.

54. Be open to refinements in your timeline after you get started, but don't get too sidetracked.

- Unless you are "called" to go in another direction altogether, stay the course and stick to your outline.
- If your mind wanders and you start writing about something else, do that in another color. When you review your work, you'll know it's just "extra writing" and can be copied and pasted into another document for another time.

55. Do research but stay on track.

- Don't get caught up in all the pages and pages of hyperlinks. Research is definitely important and some tangents can work in your favor.
- Just be aware not to get too sidetracked.
- Write.

56. Writing is not cut in stone; you have to experiment with every word, sentence, and paragraph.

- When I review my work, I sometimes see how a paragraph can fit more appropriately earlier or later in that section.
- Be open.

57. Collect stories from everyone you know.

58. Read lots of books.

- Learn from other great authors. Let your mind marinate in their words, style, and stories.

- These authors, through their works, are your mentors.

- You'll be amazed at how deeply powerful this is for you.

- I usually have 5-8 books going at a time. I will read certain kinds of books at different times of the day, or depending on my mood. By having lots of books by my side, I can always choose which book is best *when*, and I'm guaranteed to always read.

59. Don't plan the end of the book.

- I know I just said you should follow an outline, but the contents within that outline may change – including the ending.

- I didn't know what my ending would be for my autobiography until I got to the last chapter and started to write it. I knew there was "an ending," but I didn't have a clue what it would be until I started writing. Then, line by line, the next scene came to me.

- Have a plan, but be flexible. Heaven is working with you.

60. Don't worry about the title or the subtitle of your book.

- If you don't know the title of your book yet, don't worry. It will be somewhere in the body of your work.
- If you have a title already, that's great. It may be exactly what you will use. But again, be flexible.
- Remember, heaven is working with you.

61. Talk everything out with God, verbally, *and on paper*.

- God loves you and will help you from beginning to end. After all, He is the author and the finisher[ii] of *you* and everything you do.
- Don't worry if you get stalled. Try again the next day. Clarity will come.
- Be open to surprises – God loves those. They're always good, so trust Him. It'll be worth it.

"I don't know where the idea originated that memoir writing is cathartic. For me, it's always felt like playing my own neurosurgeon, sans anesthesia. As a memoirist, you have to crack your head open and examine every uncomfortable thing in there."

Koren Zailckas

62. Your first draft is *not* going to be your best work.

- Don't be hard on yourself. Your first draft may be amazing, but it won't be your best work. I'm not talking about individual sentences or paragraphs. They may be outstanding, and never get touched in the editing process.
- I'm talking about structure, grammar, pacing, flow and storytelling – and much more.
- Working on your rewrites may be time-consuming, but your work is worth it. Little by little, you're going to watch your work come to life.
- Stay humble. Even if your work is excellent, approach your project with a student's mind and a learner's heart.
- Refuse to become overconfident.

63. The opposite of #62 is also true.

- Sometimes you think your writing is horrible.
- What you think is drivel may not be. Don't judge yourself.
- Just keep writing. There's nothing to rewrite or to edit unless you've written it first.

64. Write, then rewrite.

- And rewrite.
- And rewrite.

65. Sometimes shorter is sweeter.

66. Sometimes length is strength.

- Wisdom is essential here, but don't worry about this until you're in the editing phase.
- Just write.

67. Use dialogue between the characters whenever possible.

- Dialogue brings the reader into your story and into the secret thoughts of your mind.
- If your project doesn't include dialogue, use quotations from other sources to confirm and verify your point. You can even tell a story about them and what they said in order to bring some dimension to your writing.

68. One way to keep on point is to ask yourself this question: *Is what I'm writing quotable?*

- This is especially true in dialogue.

69. When you write dialogue, don't carry on for pages and pages without some kind of scenic or sensory break.

70. When you use descriptions in between dialogue, use them as visual or sensory descriptions.

- No need to say, "he said" when it's obvious he just said it. Instead, say, "he said slowly, his eyes glaring." (Or whatever is happening in your scene.)

71. Write a really good Preface or Introduction.

72. Write a fabulous *1st* line, *1st* paragraph, and *1st* chapter.

73. Write a fabulous *last* chapter.

74. Write an unforgettable *last* paragraph.

- Write so that when you finish your last word, your reader will feel like he's saying goodbye to a good friend.

75. Review and Rewrites

- When it's time to review your work and to do the rewrites, be gentle to yourself, but be ruthless to the words.
- Go after them like the harshest critic. It will force you to refine your work with excellence.

76. Lay your ego down.

- Your ego is never as important as your work.

77. When you review what you've written, read it aloud to yourself.

- This is the best way to get a sense of the pace, cadence, rhythm and impact of your work
- You'll also catch a lot of your errors this way.
- Do most of your rewrites this way. It will save you a lot of time. It will also save a lot of your editor's time – which means it will save you more money.

78. Don't take criticisms or reviews personally.

- They're critiquing your writing, not you.

79. Get at least 3 different unbiased opinions.

- I had 50 beta readers for my autobiographical novel and hired four editors, and two proofreaders. This may be overkill for most people, but this book was so detailed and sensitive in content, and its impact so great, that I couldn't risk anything less than absolute excellence.

80. After you've finished *all* your rewrites…

- Yes, that's right, plural—you *will* do several overhauls before you're ready to show your manuscript to anyone.
- There's a fine line between excellence and perfectionism.
- You will never know what is "perfect" anyway. Everyone has his own opinion on that. So, just do your absolute best.
- Then hire a GREAT Content and Developmental Editor *first*.
- This type of editing is *not* simple proofreading.
- Proofreading can be done later, after you finish writing your properly structured story.

81. Sometimes, writing isn't fun, it's hard work.

- No matter what, stick to it.

- Keep writing.
- It will be worth it.
- You're going to deliver a beautiful creation.

82. Once you birth your baby, you're going to have to raise it.

- The work has only just begun once you birth your book. After all, if no one reads it, then your hard work is in vain.
- Now you have to start thinking about marketing. The world will need to know about your work.
- Take my other online course, *More Than Words*. It will help you tremendously.
- Promotion and marketing is a completely different industry altogether. Invest some time to learn about it.
- You can do this yourself, but be prepared – it will take a lot of your time once you enter "this world."
- You can hire digital marketers. Many offer packages and different ways you can work with them.

83. Don't talk about your book to too many people.

- This may seem counter-intuitive. You're excited and you want to share your dream with the world!
- However, the more you talk about it, the more the ideas will come out verbally, but not on paper.
- Unless you have a system to record your thoughts as you talk about them, just stick to the writing. There's plenty of time to talk about your book once it's published.
- Moreover, always talking about your book is a sneaky way to convince yourself that you're actually working on it. But you're not. You're just talking.
- Write. Again, you can talk about your book later – once it's back from the printers.

84. Don't write just about big ideas.

- Write about someone who is going after that big idea.
- Author, E.B. White once said, *"Don't write about 'man,' write about 'a man.'"*

85. Trust yourself.

86. Tell yourself the truth.

- Ask yourself: Do I really love to write?

- Some people write only to make money. That may work, but it won't be sustaining in satisfaction.
- Write because you love to write and help people.

87. Don't write because you're hiding or running away from your responsibilities, priorities, or challenging things that need your attention.

88. Don't write because you think it will make you look intelligent.

- There are lots of unintelligent books out there that only reveal their unintelligent authors.

89. Don't write because you think it will make you famous, or launch you into your industry as a guru.

- This may - or may not - happen, but it's still not the reason to write.

90. Make a positive difference with your writing.

- Your reader should always be the #1 reason to write.
- Write so you can contribute to people's lives.
- Self-serving motives – ego, money, vengeance, market domination etc. may make you money – even a lot of money - and get you a following, but this alone will never make a meaningful life.
- Writing well is about character development.
- Write because you love writing.
- Write about what you love.
- Write about what pains you.
- Write the book you want to read but haven't been able to find yet.
- Write the book you wish you could have read when you needed it most.
- Create your own genre – I did!
- The great writers of all time wrote because they loved to write. They never wrote with the intention of being the #1 bestselling author. It may have crossed their minds, but their heart was to create a masterpiece to contribute to others.

91. The world is waiting for your contribution.

- If you don't write what's in your heart today, the world could lose something really wonderful, even life-changing. Think about the masterpieces we have today. If those authors didn't write those great works, where would we be? Write your masterpiece so the world has something to share with their children and their children's children.
- So, again, please write.

"…Pursue the things you love doing and then do them so well that people can't take their eyes off of you."

Maya Angelou

"An autobiography is not about pictures; it's about stories. It's about honesty and as much truth as you can tell without coming too close to other people's privacy."

Boris Becker

5

LOOK AFTER YOURSELF!

"Some of this book—perhaps too much—has been about how I learned to do it. Much of it has been about how you can do it better. The rest of it—and perhaps the best of it—is a permission slip: you can, you should, and if you're brave enough to start, you will. Writing is magic, as much the water of life as any other creative art. The water is free. So drink. Drink and be filled up."

Stephen King

92. Drink lots of water.

- It will help you stay alert, refreshed, and thinking clearly.

93. Dress comfortably when you write.

- I often write in my pajamas. It's wonderful.

94. Keep a foam roller next to you so you can lie on it every now and then to ease the tension in your back and shoulders.

95. See your chiropractor regularly.

96. Set a timer on your phone to check your posture regularly.

97. Take regular breaks.
- I know it's difficult to stop when you're on a roll, but take breathers when you're in between thoughts. This is the best time to step away.
- Let your eyes take in the garden, the ocean, the mountains, the next building, or whatever scenery is around you.
- Exercise your eyes by looking at something distant, then something close up. Repeat this several times. You'll thank me for this one day.
- Go for short walks, have a chat with your neighbor, play with your dogs. This will help you see things with fresh eyes when you get back to it.

98. Keep a box of tissue nearby.
- You may need some tissue as you write. Having a box of it nearby will help you manage your emotions without losing the moment or the momentum by having to search for them.

99. Keep your handheld massager nearby.

- You're going to love this. I have an old one from 10 years ago called "Thumper" and it has really helped release my tight shoulder muscles.

100. Eat healthy food.

101. It's okay to have "good" (healthy) chocolate as a snack now and then.

102. Eat frequently, and in small portions to keep your metabolism and the writing momentum high.

103. Make sure your dogs (pets) are nearby for some extra love and care.

- My dogs were an amazing part of my support team. They were great listeners, happy to sit and lie by my feet, or to hug me for hours when I wrote in bed or on the couch.
- They were also great companions for me when I needed to get away and go for long walks.

104. Breathe. Deeply. Often.

105. Writing can be painful - emotionally, physically, spiritually, conceptually, financially, and relationally…keep writing.

- Be sensitive and aware of how your work may affect you. Your loved ones don't know what you're going through, so make sure you have time to process and to decompress before "re-entering" into your family world.
- Writing your story takes time and there are sacrifices to make.

106. It's worth it

6

LOOK AFTER YOUR TECHNOLOGY.

"I believe that the memoir is the novel of the 21st century; it's an amazing form that we haven't even begun to tap…we're just getting started figuring out what the rules are."
                                                    Susan Cheever

107. Take care of your computer!

- Have a professional check your computer and all its programs.
- Update your security programs and other programs you use.
- Have your computer cleaned and checked for viruses.
- Do this frequently – even once a quarter, if possible.
- Learn to love your computer or computers.
- Be kind to your gear,
- Don't swear at it, or hit it. (I've seen people do this!)
- Don't eat or drink too close to the keyboard!

LOOK AFTER YOUR TECHNOLOGY.

- Your computer is your friend and partner in your creative process.

108. Click 'Save' every few minutes!

- Seriously!
- In time, this will be second nature and you won't miss a beat.
- Protect all your hard work – save, save, save it.

109. Back everything up on your hard drive, daily.

- Active projects need a second, or even a third technical "save"—redundancy can save you a lot of time and hassle.

7

NOW WHAT?

110. Get Beta readers

- These are people you don't know from different backgrounds, ages, interests, socio-economic backgrounds etc.). to review your work.
- I had 50 of them for my autobiography.
- Depending on the size and nature of your book, you may only need a few beta readers.

111. Trust your reader(s).

- Your readers are smart. People are savvy, so don't dummy down your work and don't patronize your readers.
- There's a difference between keeping things simple and effective, and being just plain dumb.
- Write well and your readers will do the rest.

112. Get a great editor – or more.

- There are several kinds of Editors.

- I go through this in both my courses, *The Hero In You* and *More Than Words*.
    - You'll want to definitely learn about this.
- There is a short list of my favorite people at the back of this book in the reference section.

113. Get good at receiving feedback, good or bad.

114. Ignore the critics.

- Anyone and everyone can be a critic.
- There will be critics of your work – and yes, you, too. I know I said earlier the critics are only critiquing your work, but that's because I didn't want to scare you. So, I put this part at the end when you're feeling stronger and are better equipped.
- Yes, friends, there will be unkind people who may critique you personally.
- I'm sorry, but that is just life. There are all kinds of personalities out there. Don't let that stop you from writing your great work.
- Don't listen to them when they go after you personally. Think of it this way: the only reason they're critiquing your work – and you – is because your book is out there in the world!

- Chances are, for every 1 critic, there are 100 people who love your book.
- Take things in stride, and discern whether it's feedback or an attack.
- Rise above the cruel critics.

115. Great writers are priceless.

- They're great not just because they write great work, but because they stand gracefully in front of firing squads of critics.
- They believe in themselves and their message, and are willing to pay the cost for getting it out.
- They believe in their Divine calling and message so much, that regardless of the critics, they shine even brighter for writing it.
- The great writers we have today never stopped writing because of a few naysayers – or the fear of them. They wrote because of their passion and their calling to share their story and their message.
- Be a great writer.

8

KEEP GOING

116. Finish your book.

117. Get it published.

118. Market it well.

119. Get rest.

120. Start your next book.

"My life is not an autobiography. It's just music."
                                         Mary J. Blige

"If you want to write, if you want to create, you must be the most sublime fool that God ever turned out and sent rambling. You must write every single day of your life. You must read dreadful dumb books and glorious books, and let them wrestle in beautiful fights inside your head, vulgar one moment, brilliant the next. You must lurk in libraries and climb the stacks like ladders to sniff books like perfumes and wear books like hats upon your crazy heads. I wish you a wrestling match with your Creative Muse that will last a lifetime. I wish craziness and foolishness and madness upon you. May you live with hysteria, and out of it make fine stories — science fiction or otherwise. Which finally means, may you be in love every day for the next 20,000 days. And out of that love, remake a world."

Ray Bradbury

REFERENCE

Suzanne Carlson: Content and Copy Editing, Transcription. zanniebegood@gmail.com

Jed Paschall: Writing Coach and Content Writer. jedidiah@stjudestavern.org

Tiffany Vakilian: Content and Development Editor, Publishing Consultant, Virtual Assistant. Tiffany@tiffanyvakilian.com

ABOUT THE AUTHOR

Manna began her career as an entrepreneur in the 1980s, and within a very short time, she gained national recognition for her work. In the 1990s, she and her son moved to the United States, where she used her giftings and expertise to help others in the marketplace, providing progressive marketing concepts, effective office systems, integrative team building curricula, personal and professional leadership consulting, and strategic partnerships to other small businesses around the country.

As a prolific Author, International Speaker, Trainer, Counseling/Life and Business Coach, Leader, Visionary, CEO and founder of several companies, and strategic partner to many others, Manna is passionate about helping people step into their calling, live extraordinary lives, prosper through chaos, be a forerunner with unseen opportunities, lead under pressure, and deliver results. Conventional models teach us to gather more information; Manna teaches us to develop wisdom. In this way, not only will the individual prosper, but the entire community will prosper.

Manna earned an MA in Psychology, a Ph.D. in Philosophy, and additional certifications as a Holistic Health Practitioner (HHP), a Certified Clinical Nutritionist (CCN), and a Certified Clinical Herbalist

(CCH), among many others.

Now with over twenty-seven years of entrepreneurial experience, she has spoken to over 40,000 people, worked with hundreds of different businesses and organizations, guided even more individuals seeking personal excellence, and has taught to private writer's groups in Oxford, England. She has clients in nine countries, has contributed to numerous educational, disciplinary and advisory boards, is the Lead Trainer and Editor in Chief for KWA (Kingdom Writer's Association) and is an Ordained Leader with Third Day Churches. She is also a marathon runner, a health and exercise enthusiast, an avid reader, is conversant in four languages, plays tennis and the piano, studied martial arts, and is active in her community.

Manna and her family live in San Diego, California.

WHAT'S YOUR STORY?

Since the publication of my Made For More™, many people have asked me to help them write their story, too.

Saying *I'm Made For More™* isn't just a catchy affirmation; it is a statement of truth. In fact, it's so true that when you say it, your heart exhales with relief and excitement! After years of study, coaching, teaching, and training, I finally published my book, **Made For More™** in 2015. Shortly after that, I launched my Made For More™ course.

THE NEXT CHAPTER…

My story continues—but now the adventures are bigger, better, and bolder!

Find out more about what we're doing, the fascinating people I'm meeting, and the beautiful souls whose lives are turned around because they decided they were *Made For More™!*

Connect with me to see what city we'll be speaking in next, what new courses are coming up, and what new books are being published.

Find Manna online at www.mannaforlife.com
www.facebook.com/mannaforlife
Twitter @Mannaforlife
Instagram @Mannaforlife

LinkedIn at Manna Ko

I'm looking forward to meeting you soon! God bless you!

---

[i] 1 Corinthians 2:9 NLT
[ii] Hebrews 12:2

www.ingramcontent.com/pod-product-compliance
Lightning Source LLC
LaVergne TN
LVHW020939090426
835512LV00020B/3434